DO MATH WITH SPORTS STATS!

FOOTBALL

Stats, Facts, and Figures

BY KATE MIKOLEY

Gareth Stevens
PUBLISHING

Please visit our website, www.garethstevens.com. For a free color catalog of all our high-quality books, call toll free 1-800-542-2595 or fax 1-877-542-2596.

Library of Congress Cataloging-in-Publication Data

Names: Mikoley, Kate, author.
Title: Football : stats, facts, and figures / Kate Mikoley.
Description: New York : Gareth Stevens Publishing, 2018. | Series: Do math with sports stats! | Includes index.
Identifiers: LCCN 2017031767| ISBN 9781538211335 (pbk.) | ISBN 9781538211342 (6 pack) | ISBN 9781538211359 (library bound)
Subjects: LCSH: Football–Juvenile literature. | Mathematics–Juvenile literature.
Classification: LCC GV950.7 .M47 2018 | DDC 796.332–dc23
LC record available at https://lccn.loc.gov/2017031767

First Edition

Published in 2018 by
Gareth Stevens Publishing
111 East 14th Street, Suite 349
New York, NY 10003

Copyright © 2018 Gareth Stevens Publishing

Designer: Samantha DeMartin
Editor: Kate Mikoley

Photo credits: pp. 4–29 (paperclips) AVS-Images/Shutterstock.com; covers, pp. 1–29 (pencil) irin-k/Shutterstock.com; pp. 4–29 (post-its) Pixel Embargo/Shutterstock.com; pp. 4–29 (tape) Flas100/Shutterstock.com; pp. 3–32 (graph paper) BLACKDAY/Shutterstock.com; covers, pp. 1–32 (bleacher texture) Al Sermeno Photography/Shutterstock.com; covers, pp. 1–29 (clipboard) Mega Pixel/Shutterstock.com; covers, pp. 1–29 (formula overlay) lolya1988/Shutterstock.com; covers, pp. 1–29 (index card) photastic/Shutterstock.com; cover, p. 1 Eugene Onischenko/Shutterstock.com; p. 5 Steve Broer/Shutterstock.com; p. 7 (Super Bowl) Ezra Shaw/Getty Images Sport/Getty Images; pp. 7 (Rose Bowl), 10 Harry How/Getty Images Sport/Getty Images; p. 8 enterlinedesign/Shutterstock.com; pp. 9, 24 Elsa/Getty Images Sport/Getty Images; p. 11 Thearon W. Henderson/Getty Images Sport/Getty Images; p. 13 Jonathan Daniel/Getty Images Sport/Getty Images; p. 15 (main) Kevin C. Cox/Getty Images Sport/Getty Images; p. 15 (background) mexrix/Shutterstock.com; p. 16 Doug Pensinger/Getty Images Sport/Getty Images; p. 17 Jeff Gross/Getty Images Sport/Getty Images; p. 18 Brett Carlsen/Getty Images Sport/Getty Images; p. 19 Hannah Foslien/Getty Images Sport/Getty Images; p. 20 Jonathan Bachman/Getty Images Sport/Getty Images; p. 21 Al Bello/Getty Images Sport/Getty Images; p. 23 (main) Maddie Meyer/Getty Images Sport/Getty Images; p. 23 (background) Billion Photos/Shutterstock.com; p. 25 Jim Rogash/Getty Images Sport/Getty Images; p. 27 Andy Lyons/Getty Images Sport/Getty Images; p. 29 Justin Edmonds/Getty Images Sport/Getty Images.

Printed in the United States of America

CPSIA compliance information: Batch #CW18GS: For further information contact Gareth Stevens, New York, New York at 1-800-542-2595.

CONTENTS

Words in the glossary appear in **bold** type the first time they are used in the text.

KICK OFF THE GAME!

Thousands of screaming fans pack the stadium. Twenty-two men wearing pullover shirts called jerseys that cover bulky shoulder pads take the field. Each player gets in position, and the ball is placed on a tee. When an official blows the whistle, one player runs forward and kicks the ball into the air. The game has begun!

A COLLEGE GAME

Football got its start in the 1800s at colleges in the United States. The creators of the game combined parts of soccer and **rugby** to form gridiron football, the game played all over the United States today. It's also sometimes called American football because in many countries, soccer is called football.

Football is one of the most popular sports in the United States, where millions of people watch **professional** games every year. Math plays a key role in the game. Numbers are everywhere in football—from the lines on the field to the score on the board.

THE WORD "GRIDIRON" WAS USED TO DESCRIBE AMERICAN FOOTBALL BECAUSE THE LINES ON THE FIELD LOOK LIKE A GRIDIRON, A TOOL USED FOR COOKING OVER A FIRE.

COING PRO

The National Football League (NFL) is the major professional football organization in the United States. It began in 1920, although it was originally called the American Professional Football Association. Today, the NFL is made up of 32 teams split into two conferences—the National Football Conference (NFC) and the American Football Conference (AFC).

Though the game has grown in popularity and changed over the years, football is still particularly popular where it began—in colleges and universities around the United States. Many NFL players got their start by playing for their high school and college teams!

THE NUMBERS GAME

THE NFC AND THE AFC EACH HAVE 16 TEAMS. WITHIN EACH CONFERENCE THERE ARE 4 DIVISIONS, OR SMALLER GROUPS. IF EACH DIVISION HAS AN EQUAL NUMBER OF TEAMS, WHAT EQUATION WOULD YOU USE TO FIGURE OUT HOW MANY TEAMS ARE IN EACH DIVISION? CAN YOU SOLVE THE EQUATION?

ANSWER ON PAGE 29.

BIG FOOTBALL GAMES ARE OFTEN CALLED BOWLS. THE SUPER BOWL IS THE CHAMPIONSHIP GAME OF THE NFL. COLLEGE FOOTBALL HAS MANY BOWLS, SUCH AS THE ROSE BOWL, ORANGE BOWL, AND SUGAR BOWL.

WELCOME TO THE ROSE BOWL GAME

Rose Bowl

Super Bowl

KNOW THE BASICS

Football fields are measured in yards. The field is 100 yards (91.4 m) long and 53.33 yards (48.8 m) wide. Each end has a goal line and an end zone. Each end zone is 10 yards (9.1 m), making the length of the entire field 120 yards (109.6 m). At the end of each end zone are the goalposts.

White yard lines cross the field every 5 yards. The lines are numbered every 10 yards up to 50 starting from each end zone. The 50-yard line marks the middle of the field.

Robert Alford runs the ball down the field.

THE NUMBERS GAME

THE AREA OF A RECTANGLE IS **CALCULATED** BY MULTIPLYING THE LENGTH
TIMES THE WIDTH. THAT MEANS THE AREA OF A FOOTBALL FIELD, NOT
COUNTING THE END ZONES, IS ABOUT 5,333 SQUARE YARDS! WHAT'S THE AREA
OF A RECTANGLE THAT'S 12 YARDS BY 23 YARDS? ANSWER ON PAGE 29.

In football, each team has 11 players on the field at a time. The team that has possession of the ball is called the offense. Their job is to get the ball down the field and into the end zone either by throwing it or running with it.

Jonathan Stewart dives for a touchdown.

A TOUCHDOWN IS SCORED WHEN THE OFFENSE GETS THE BALL ACROSS THE OTHER TEAM'S GOAL LINE AND INTO THE END ZONE. A TOUCHDOWN IS WORTH 6 POINTS!

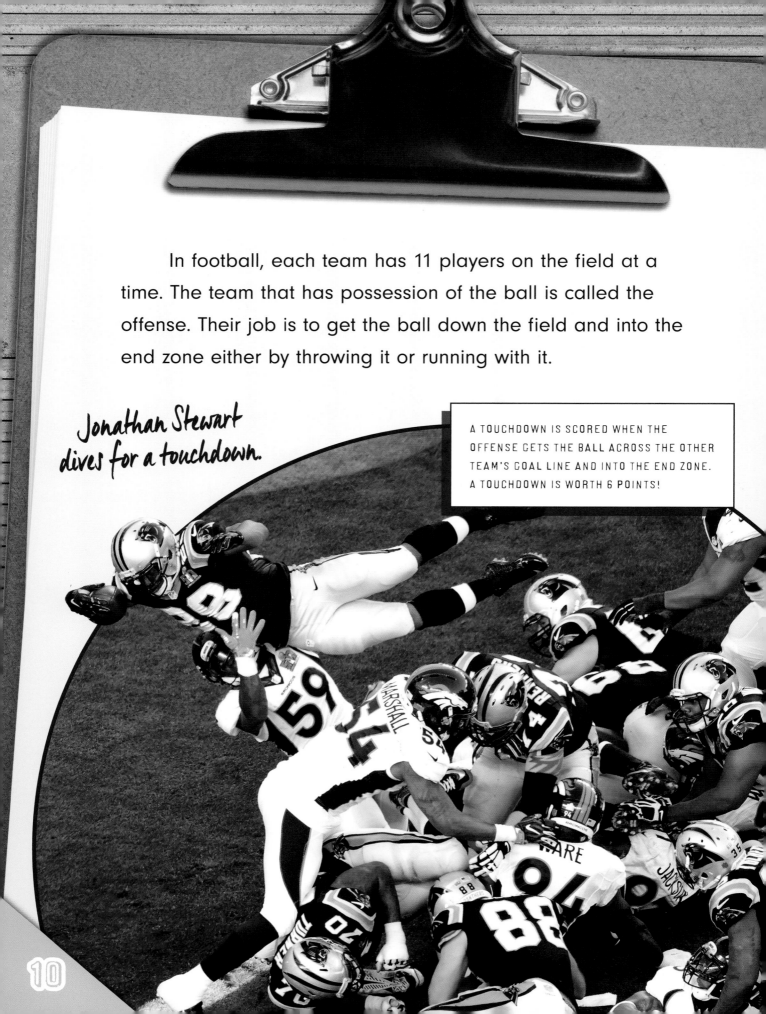

The other team is called the defense. They try to stop the offense from making it to the end zone and scoring. They often do this by tackling the player with the ball, recovering a **fumble**, or **intercepting** a pass. When the offense scores or loses possession of the ball, the teams switch roles.

Richard Sherman intercepts the ball.

STATS AND SKILLS

Statistics, or stats, are numbers that show how well a player or team is doing at a certain skill. In every game, teams have to play both offense and defense. Different stats show how well particular players and teams perform each role and the different skills that go into them.

GETTING POINTS

After a touchdown, the scoring team can attempt to make a conversion. This is a chance to gain extra points by either kicking the ball through the goalposts or carrying the ball across the goal line. A successful kick gets the scoring team 1 point, while carrying the ball across the goal line gets them 2 points.

The offensive team can also score points by kicking a field goal. This is often done when a team can't score a touchdown. A field goal is worth 3 points. Defensive teams can score points through **safeties**.

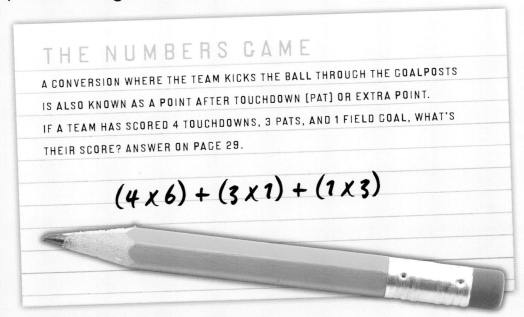

THE NUMBERS GAME

A CONVERSION WHERE THE TEAM KICKS THE BALL THROUGH THE GOALPOSTS IS ALSO KNOWN AS A POINT AFTER TOUCHDOWN (PAT) OR EXTRA POINT. IF A TEAM HAS SCORED 4 TOUCHDOWNS, 3 PATS, AND 1 FIELD GOAL, WHAT'S THEIR SCORE? ANSWER ON PAGE 29.

$$(4 \times 6) + (3 \times 1) + (1 \times 3)$$

KICKING A BALL THAT'S HELD IN A STILL, UPRIGHT POSITION IS CALLED PLACE-KICKING. THE PLACE KICKER, SOMETIMES JUST CALLED THE KICKER, KICKS FIELD GOALS AND KICKOFFS.

Mason Crosby kicks a field goal.

A FRACTIONS GAME

Football games are divided into quarters. In the NFL and college football, quarters are 15 minutes each, meaning a standard game has 60 minutes of play. But games last much longer than 60 minutes. The clock stops for many reasons throughout the game, including time-outs and **penalties**. There are also breaks between quarters, with a longer halftime break after the second quarter.

If the game is tied at the end of the fourth quarter, it goes into overtime. Overtime was added in the NFL in 1974. In 2017, the NFL shortened the length of the overtime period from 15 minutes to 10.

THE NUMBERS GAME

IN THE NFL, THE REGULAR SEASON IS 17 WEEKS LONG AND EACH TEAM PLAYS 16 GAMES. THAT'S BECAUSE EACH TEAM GETS A WEEK OFF, CALLED A BYE WEEK. IF EACH GAME HAS 4 QUARTERS, HOW MANY TOTAL QUARTERS DOES A TEAM PLAY OVER A FULL SEASON? ANSWER ON PAGE 29.

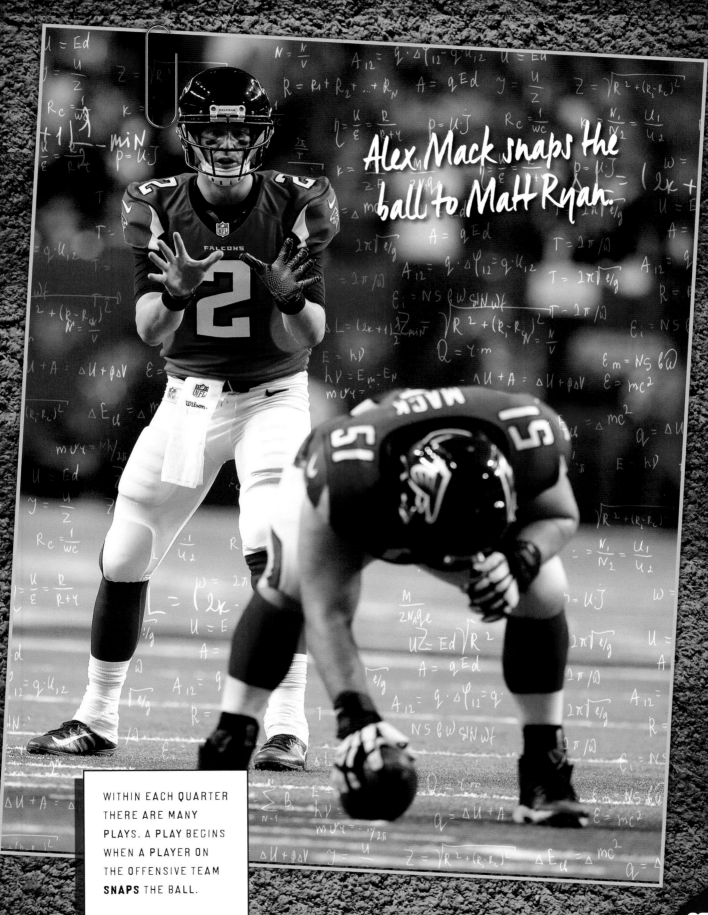

Alex Mack snaps the ball to Matt Ryan.

WITHIN EACH QUARTER THERE ARE MANY PLAYS. A PLAY BEGINS WHEN A PLAYER ON THE OFFENSIVE TEAM **SNAPS** THE BALL.

GAIN SOME YARDS!

When a team has the ball, they get four downs, or chances, to move the ball 10 yards. If they successfully gain the 10 yards, they get a new set of four downs and get to keep the ball. If they don't, the other team gets the ball.

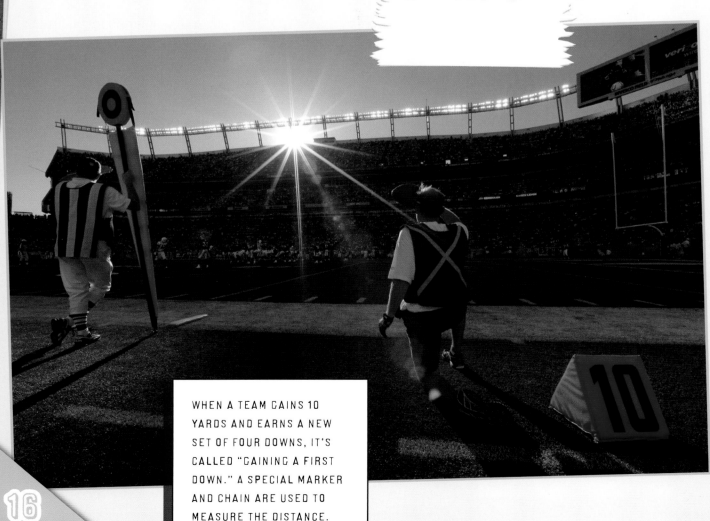

WHEN A TEAM GAINS 10 YARDS AND EARNS A NEW SET OF FOUR DOWNS, IT'S CALLED "GAINING A FIRST DOWN." A SPECIAL MARKER AND CHAIN ARE USED TO MEASURE THE DISTANCE.

The third down is very important. If a team has made it to a third down, they may be getting close to the end of their turn. They need to either gain the 10 yards or score. A team's ability to do this is measured by a stat called third down efficiency or conversion rate.

Antonio Gates makes a catch.

THE NUMBERS GAME

THIRD DOWN EFFICIENCY IS A PERCENTAGE. IT TAKES INTO ACCOUNT THE TOTAL ATTEMPTED THIRD DOWNS AND THE CONVERTED THIRD DOWNS. IN 2013, THE CHARGERS HAD THIRD DOWN EFFICIENCY OF 49 PERCENT. HOW MANY FACTORS OF 49 ARE THERE? WHAT ARE THEY? REMEMBER, FACTORS ARE NUMBERS YOU CAN MULTIPLY TOGETHER TO GET ANOTHER NUMBER.

ANSWER ON PAGE 29.

One way a team can advance the ball down the field or get a touchdown is by a player running with the ball. This is called rushing. Rushing yards is a stat that measures how far a player runs with the ball during a play. Running backs and quarterbacks are often the players who score rushing touchdowns.

For professional football players, a good rushing yard total for a single game is 100 yards or more. Throughout an entire season, a good running back will often rush more than 1,000 yards!

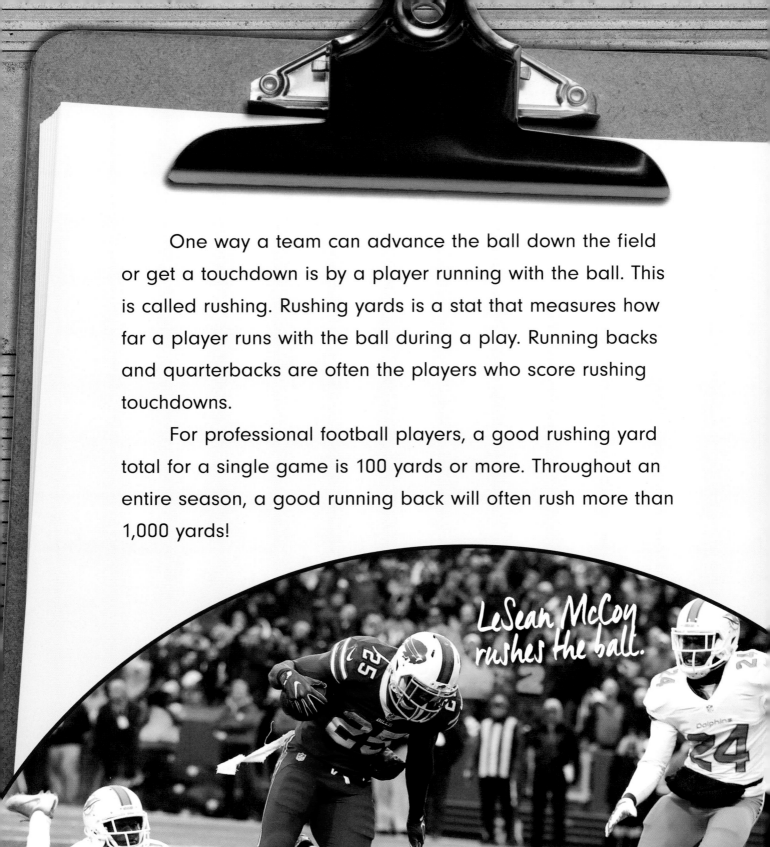

LeSean McCoy rushes the ball.

THE NUMBERS GAME

IN 2015, ADRIAN PETERSON PLAYED 16 GAMES FOR THE MINNESOTA VIKINGS. HE RUSHED 1,485 YARDS AND MADE 11 RUSHING TOUCHDOWNS. IF A PLAYER RUSHED 580 YARDS, HOW MANY FEET DOES THAN MEAN THEY RUSHED? REMEMBER, THERE ARE 3 FEET IN A YARD. ANSWER ON PAGE 29.

IN HIS FIRST SEASON PLAYING FOR THE NFL, PETERSON RUSHED 296 YARDS IN A SINGLE GAME!

If the offense isn't running with the ball, they're probably throwing it. A pass is considered complete when another player on the same team catches the ball. If the ball hits the ground before someone catches it, it's considered an incomplete pass. Forward passes are only allowed from behind the **line of scrimmage**.

Drew Brees

IN THE 2016 NFL SEASON, DREW BREES HAD HIS FIFTH SEASON IN WHICH HE PASSED MORE THAN 5,000 YARDS. NO OTHER NFL PLAYER HAD REACHED THAT MARK MORE THAN ONCE!

THE NUMBERS GAME

SOME QUARTERBACKS HAVE PASSED MORE THAN 500 YARDS IN A SINGLE GAME! LET'S SAY A PLAYER PASSED 100 YARDS IN BOTH THE FIRST AND SECOND QUARTERS OF A GAME. IN THE THIRD QUARTER, THEY PASSED 60 YARDS. IN THE FOURTH QUARTER, THEY PASSED 120 YARDS. HOW MANY TOTAL YARDS DID THEY PASS? ANSWER ON PAGE 29.

Andrew Luck makes a pass.

The quarterback usually does the most passing. Yards gained by passing, or passing yards, is an important stat for quarterbacks. Quarterbacks are often considered great if they pass more than 4,000 yards in a season, but a few have passed more than 5,000 yards in a season!

COMPLETE THE PASS

A quarterback can throw the ball many times, but if the pass isn't completed, the yards don't count. That's why pass completion is also important. This just means that a pass is successfully caught by a player on the same team. The player who catches the ball is called a receiver and gets a **reception** each time they legally catch the ball. Receivers' stats are also measured in yards.

Completion percentage shows how well a quarterback is doing at completing his forward pass attempts. This is figured out by finding the total percentage of pass attempts that are completed.

THE NUMBERS GAME

TO FIND A PLAYER'S COMPLETION PERCENTAGE, YOU NEED TO KNOW HOW MANY TOTAL PASSES THEY'VE ATTEMPTED AND HOW MANY OF THOSE HAVE BEEN COMPLETED. LET'S SAY A PLAYER ATTEMPTED 200 PASSES IN A SEASON. OF THESE, 3/4 WERE COMPLETED. HOW MANY COMPLETED PASSES DOES THE PLAYER HAVE? ANSWER ON PAGE 29.

$$200 \times \frac{3}{4}$$

IN THE 2016 POSTSEASON, OR GAMES PLAYED AFTER THE REGULAR SEASON, TOM BRADY HAD 93 COMPLETIONS AND A COMPLETION PERCENTAGE OF 65.5!

TACKLING

When the offense is trying to get the ball down the field, the defense's goal is to stop them. When a player on the defense catches a pass thrown by the offense, it's called an interception. The ball can also be stopped by tackling the player who's holding it.

DANGER ON THE FIELD

In its early years, football was a very dangerous sport. The game was **violent**, and people didn't wear the kind of protective gear they wear today. Some players died, and many more were injured. People still get hurt playing football today, but thanks to changes in the rules and modern gear, it's safer than it once was.

Clay Matthews sacks Kirk Cousins.

Tackling a player while they're behind the line of scrimmage and before they've thrown a forward pass is called sacking. The quarterback is the most likely player to get sacked. If a player is sacked or tackled in their own end zone, the defense gets a safety and earns 2 points.

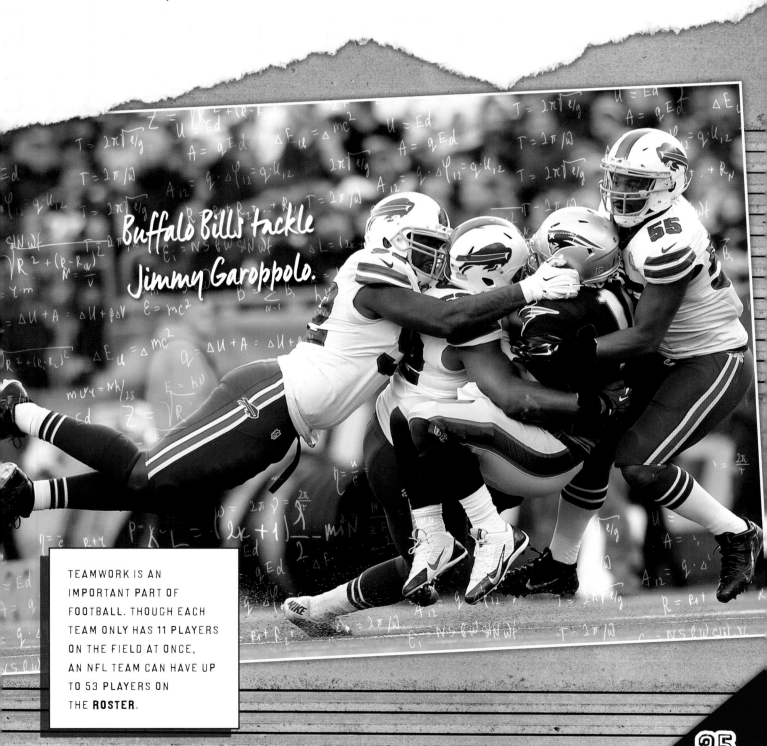

Buffalo Bills tackle Jimmy Garoppolo.

TEAMWORK IS AN IMPORTANT PART OF FOOTBALL. THOUGH EACH TEAM ONLY HAS 11 PLAYERS ON THE FIELD AT ONCE, AN NFL TEAM CAN HAVE UP TO 53 PLAYERS ON THE **ROSTER**.

MODERNIZING
THE STATS

Stats have been tracked in many different sports for years, but people are constantly coming up with new stats and ways to find them. In the NFL, players wear special sensors, or tools that detect changes in elements such as speed and movement. These sensors provide special stats called next-gen stats.

Next-gen stats are often more specific and tailored to the individual player than many other stats in football. They measure things such as how far the ball travels on a pass and how fast a person carrying the ball runs. This **technology** also charts a player's movements on the field.

NEW INFORMATION

Next-gen stats often take into account information that other stats do not. For example, longest plays is a stat measured by next-gen stats that takes into account the total distance the ball carrier travels during a play. This includes their total movement around the field, not just the yards they've gained.

NEXT-GEN STATS ARE FAIRLY NEW TO THE NFL. MANY PEOPLE BELIEVE REGULAR STATS ARE STILL BETTER AT SHOWING THE TRUE ABILITIES OF A PLAYER.

LOOKING AT THE NUMBERS

Many football fans use stats to create their own football teams! In fantasy football, people pick real NFL players to play on pretend teams. Points are earned based on how well the actual players do in the real games they play. People who play fantasy football often look at players' stats when deciding whom they want to play on their team.

While stats are important, they aren't the only things that matter in the game. A team can have great overall stats and still lose. A team's performance can make or break the game. In the end, points scored is the most important stat.

JERSEY NUMBERS

In football, even the number on a player's jersey means something! In the NFL, certain positions wear numbers within a specific range. For example, quarterbacks wear numbers between 1 and 19. Teams sometimes even retire the numbers of their best players. This means future players won't wear that number.

p. 6 – equation: 16 ÷ 4 ;
    answer: 4 teams

p. 9 – 276 square yards

p. 12 – 30 points

p. 14 – 64 quarters

p. 17 – 3 factors; 1, 7, 49

p. 19 – 1,740 feet

p. 21 – 380 yards

p. 22 – 150 completed passes

IN 2013, THE DENVER BRONCOS BECAME THE FIRST NFL TEAM TO SCORE MORE THAN 600 POINTS IN A SINGLE SEASON, SCORING A TOTAL OF 606 POINTS.

GLOSSARY

calculate: to figure something out using math

fumble: to drop the football while it's still in play

intercept: to take control of a pass that was meant for a player on the other team

line of scrimmage: an imaginary line on the field where the football is put before each play begins

penalty: a loss for breaking a rule

professional: earning money from an activity that many people do for fun

reception: the statistic that counts the number of times a player has caught a pass

roster: the list of people that are on a team

rugby: a game similar to football in which each team tries to carry or kick a ball over the other team's goal line

safety: a score of 2 points for the defensive team when an offensive player who has the ball is tackled behind his own team's goal line

snap: to send the ball back to the quarterback

technology: the practical application of specialized knowledge

violent: having to do with the use of force to harm someone

FOR MORE INFORMATION

BOOKS

Kortemeier, Todd. *Pro Football by the Numbers.* North Mankato, MN: Capstone Press, 2016.

Mahaney, Ian F. *The Math of Football.* New York, NY: PowerKids Press, 2012.

WEBSITES

Next Gen Leaders
www.nfl.com/stats/ngs/leaders
Use this site to keep up with the NFL's latest next-gen statistics.

Pro Football Reference
www.pro-football-reference.com/
Find up-to-date stats and figures about your favorite players and teams here.

INDEX